I0461393

Breaking the Habit of Mom Guilt

7 Steps to Finding Inner Strength and Peace

Shila Marie

Published by: SR PUBLISHING LLC
1308 Stockton Hill Rd #159
Kingman, AZ 86401
Contact: info@TheMaskedPoet.org

All illustrations and images are the property of SR Publishing LLC

Content Editor: David Strauss
Book Design: Barbara Wade
Author Coaching: David Strauss

ORDERING INFORMATION:

Special discounts are available on quantity purchases by corporations, associations, and organizations. Contact the publisher at the above address for special discounts.

Dedicated to my daughters
Brynlee & Brooklyn, Bryan,
and my parents, Joel, and Amy.

DISCLAIMER

This book is presented solely for educational and entertainment purposes only. The author and publisher are not offering it as a substitute for professional advice. It is not intended to replace a one-on-one relationship with a qualified mental health care professional.

Neither the author nor the publisher shall be held liable or responsible to any person or entity with respect to any loss or incidents or consequential damages caused or alleged to have been caused, directly or indirectly, by the information contained herein.

Every person is different, and the suggested strategies contained herein may not be suitable for each unique situation.

Table of Contents

Introduction

"I've got a bad case of the 3:00 am guilts—
you know, when you lie in bed awake and replay all those things
you didn't do right? Because, as we all know, nothing solves insomnia
like a nice warm glass of regret, depression, and self-loathing."

—D.D. Barant, *Dying Bites*

Hey, girl—hey!

Do you suffer from Mom Guilt?

You know what I'm talking about. It's that feeling that no matter what you do as a mother, it is never enough. Not because someone told you that, but because you feel the guilt in the pit of your stomach that you should have or could have done more.

Do you love being a mother but still dream of something more than changing diapers, watching cartoons, and changing your shirt five times a day from spit-up?

Do you feel like you lost your identity when you became a mom, or maybe just miss the girl you used to be?

Do you feel like you are spread too thin between all the hats you wear throughout the day, week, month, and year?

Do you want to enjoy being a mom and not feel like you should be doing more?

I think you get it. If you suffer from any form of Mom Guilt or want to get your life back while still being there for your kids, then this book is for you.

I wrote this book because Mom Guilt was eating me alive from the inside out, and I knew there were other moms just like me who needed help—and I had to do something about it. I had to take an honest and close look at my life to understand the roots of this whole Mom Guilt emotional trap so that I could work through it and then challenge other moms to do the same by starting *The Mom Guilt Movement.*

This book is the blueprint for *The Mom Guilt Movement.* It is not a "feel good" book, nor is it about how to be a better mother. There are more than enough parenting books out there. This is about how to be a better you while being the best mom you can be.

There are millions of messages out there about how amazing motherhood is. You don't need to hear me tell you that because I know you already know that part. I am here to talk about the hard parts, the dark parts. I want to bring them into the light and normalize the truth that—although being a mom is the greatest job and title we will ever have; it is also one of the hardest.

The reality is that we cannot find peace if we are pretending that we are not suffering. *The Mom Guilt Movement* is about giving you permission to stop pretending and the courage to start healing.

The goal of the movement is to give you the insight and strength to liberate you from yourself. This will be accomplished by using the following seven steps to break the habit of Mom Guilt:

1) Find your center
2) Keep your word
3) Stop playing the victim
4) Fill your cup first
5) It takes a village
6) Join the challenge
7) Invite a friend

Each of these steps is like mini guide stones that will lead you toward inner peace and strength.

Everything that I share has been through the filter of my life. If it worked for me, it could also work for you. So, as you join me on this journey, I am asking you to take off your emotional guard so that we can rediscover our strength together.

I make this promise to you. When you finish reading this book, you will have the insight and tools to reclaim your life while still being the best possible mom for your kids.

I recommend reading this book twice. First, read it to understand the overall message. Second, read and study it as a self-improvement tool. Either way, I want to encourage you to go all in. Read every page and be present for every story. Not for the sake of me—hoping that you read my whole book—but because my true wish is that every person who consumes what I have written can take something away, that will be meaningful and transformational.

Through this book, my blog, podcast, and my social media groups, my vision is to help at least ten thousand moms become aware of solutions to overcome feelings of Mom Guilt—by helping them find their inner strenght and peace.

Part One | Mom Guilt

Chapter 1

Making Myself Vulnerable

*"Perhaps this is the moment
for which you've been created."*

—Esther 4:14

Before we get into the Mom Guilt Challenge, I want to open up to you and share some of the hardships I have worked through which brought me to the point of writing this book.

The reason I share this is because you and I have a lot more in common than just being moms. Each of us has persevered through difficulties that have defined who we are. I want you to know that you are not alone in your pain. No struggle is any better or worse than another. We each have our strengths and weaknesses and, ultimately, the choice is ours to either learn and grow from our experiences or to give up and shrivel up.

In November of 2020 I asked myself two questions:
1) What is my true identity?
2) What is my purpose?

I was in the middle of reading *100 Days to Brave* by Annie Downs, and I found myself in a mental and emotional tailspin. I never knew it was okay to just be me. After growing up with unimaginable amounts of mental and emotional turbulence, my idea of normal would scare most people.

My parents were in their late teens when I was born. As you can imagine, because they were so young, they didn't have the experience or maturity to raise a young girl. Though it wasn't intentional on their part, feeling unworthy, rejected, and betrayed was all I knew because of the environment in which I was raised.

The sound of gunshots in the house, drugs, alcohol, living room tattoos, and abuse was my version of normal. My father had his own challenges, which prevented him from participating in my life and attending to my emotional needs as a young girl. Watching my father leave when I was three years old and then being raised by a teen mother had its consequences—many of which showed up as Mom Guilt after I had my first child.

Luckily for me, my mother always did the best she could—given the difficult circumstances during my childhood. She has always been my best friend, and we were able to get through so many difficulties together.

We were blessed when my mom married her new husband, Joel, who helped to set aside a lot of the emotional pressure and difficulties that were weighing us down. It's incredible how one person can change everything. My whole world as a child shifted for the better because of Joel.

Later in life, I found myself facing a whole new set of difficulties. My struggles with relationships and infertility lead to a divorce. Then, after I was told that I was infertile, I became pregnant by my new fiancé less than a year into our relationship. If that were not enough, I was diagnosed with skin cancer. All of this led me to use alcohol and overspending to cope with my difficulties.

As you can imagine, with a child on the way, my relationship with my fiancé changed very quickly. We became parents before we fully got to know each other. Nonetheless, we gladly accepted responsibility for our beautiful child—which I now see as a surprise gift from God. We've had many unforeseen challenges both as parents and as husband and wife, which contributed to my wanting to write this book.

God gave me a beautiful daughter and, in turn, forced me to reconcile my childhood emotional turmoil. The good news is that I am no longer stuck in that struggle linked to my early years. My new normal has changed so much because I stopped trying to be "normal" and accepted just being me. I was able to find my center amidst it all, and I want you to be able to make that transformation as well.

While reading *100 Days to Brave*, I rediscovered my relationship with God. I gained the courage and confidence to put my past behind me and move forward in a healthier direction. That mental, emotional, and spiritual shift contributed to my courage and willingness to address my feelings of Mom Guilt head-on.

I no longer see myself as a victim because I discovered how to turn my pain into power. I realized that your pain makes you stronger if you learn from the experiences. However, that strength isn't worth much if you are not brave enough to flex it and take control of your life.

I know that I am not alone in my struggles with abuse, trauma, and marital issues. There are plenty of moms who have buried their stories because they are afraid of resurfacing the pain, being judged, or they don't have the courage to get help.

I also know that any feelings of Mom Guilt have roots in our own feelings of inadequacy that preceded becoming a mom. Having a kid is like placing a magnifying glass over your emotional vulnerabilities. They were always there, but now they have come to the surface because of the emotional demands of being a mom.

For those of you who are hiding your struggles and sense that it is affecting you as a mom, my wish for you is that my story will touch you in some way and help you figure out who you truly are.

You cannot heal anything that you hide. You must find the strength to not live as a victim and instead embrace your superpower as a mom. You want to learn to use your pain to become stronger and wiser. This is important for you and your kid because your kid inherits and models your emotional patterns and beliefs. You are their mental, emotional, and spiritual teacher, either directly or inadvertently, through the example of your life.

Perhaps Mom Guilt is not just about our children but also the guilt of unresolved emotions that carry over from pain that we have suppressed or denied.

Now that you know a bit about who I am and why I wrote this book let's shift our focus and take a closer look at the five stages of Mom Guilt.

Chapter 2

Five Phases of Mom Guilt

*"The realities of motherhood are often obscured by a halo of illusions.
The future mother tends to fantasize about love and happiness
and overlooks the other aspects of child-rearing: the exhaustion,
frustration, loneliness, and even depression,
with its attendant state of guilt."*

—Lisabeth Badinter

Every mom has their version and unique experience with Mom Guilt. We know what a mom is, but what is Mom Guilt?

My definition of Mom Guilt is easily understood by any mom:

> "A feeling of regret, shame, responsibility, embarrassment, or remorse for not having done something correctly, or to the best of your ability, or for violating your personal standards—whether the feeling is real or imagined."

Mom Guilt is clearly an emotion, not an action or behavior. I would go so far as to say that Mom Guilt is not a good or bad emotion. Rather, it is there to serve as a course correction.

When you are feeling Mom Guilt, it is your inner voice telling you that you could do better or that somehow, you have fallen short of your true capability. Mom Guilt can also be the result of unrealistic expectations of yourself. Even though you can only do the best you can with what you have, it's still easy to fall into the pattern of feeling unrealistically guilty.

Mom Guilt is very powerful. You cannot describe how it feels, but as soon as you mention the words, you instantly have a memory of the feeling from something in the past or something that you are avoiding. Yes, avoidance is a form of guilt.

"I would feel very guilty if I did that."

That guilty feeling, which is like none other, is most obvious when you flat out make a bad decision, and the result is staring you in the face. You can only hope that no one was watching to avoid the shame that comes with guilt.

To be sure that Mom Guilt is a universal emotion with common characteristics, I interviewed nearly one hundred moms ranging from twenty years old to sixty-six years old. Each of them can remember feeling Mom Guilt for the first time—either during pregnancy or within the first month of becoming a mother.

What does this tell us about moms? There's one thing for sure that every mom will agree on, and that is that the first month after giving birth has a very steep learning curve. It's sort of an emotional maze with little traps along the way designed to test your strength and build your patience.

Based on my interpretation of all those interviews, I have segmented Mom Guilt into five phases.

Five Phases of Mom Guilt
1) Infant / Baby
2) Toddler/ Preschooler
3) School age
4) Adolescent / Teen
5) Adult

Each phase progresses to a new type of Mom Guilt. For some, it gets worse; for others it lightens up a bit over time. For the ones who said they feel less guilt now, the change was not due to the age of their child, but rather the personal growth they experienced. They also learned to forgive themselves and manage their lives more productively.

So far, I have not found a single mom that has never felt even a little Mom Guilt—ever.

Here are some paraphrased examples of each stage of Mom Guilt based on real interviews.

Phase 1 – Infant/Baby

This phase is where most moms first remember feeling guilt. Some mothers even noticed it during pregnancy.

MOM 1: I felt guilty as soon as I found out I was pregnant out of wedlock.

MOM 2: As soon as I found out my baby had a developmental issue, I felt guilty because I began to question whether I had done something wrong to cause it.

MOM 3: I felt guilty from day one because everyone told me that it's no longer about me. Just do what is best for my child. As a result, all I have ever known and believed is that being a mom means personal sacrifice.

Phase 2 – Toddler/Preschooler

This phase is a whole new level of Mom Guilt. You question if your kid is learning enough, getting enough attention, enough love, enough structure, enough of everything.

MOM 4: I struggle with Mom Guilt because my twins never get to have mommy or daddy to themselves. When I do something for one of them, the other feels left out and gets jealous. "I feel like I just can't win."

Phase 3 – School Age

This phase of Mom Guilt gets even harder because the children start to pick up on more outside influences from other kids, TV shows, and social media. This tends to play a large role in Mom Guilt.

MOM 5: It is so hard to parent at this age because you hear a lot of painful words from your kids.

"That's not fair."

"I hate you."

"You are ruining my life."

"All of my friends get to ____, why can't I?"

You start to question yourself as a mother. "Am I being too harsh on my kids."

MOM 6: Mothering at this age has you wondering if you are helping or hurting them by trying to keep them young and innocent as long as possible.

Phase 4 – Adolescent/ Teen

This age is when they start wanting more freedom and space but also don't want to take on any extra responsibility.

MOM 7: I want to give my kids the freedom to figure out who they are, but also need to be a responsible parent and keep them safe and well-informed. "It feels almost impossible to do both."

Phase 5 – Adult

This phase is very difficult because your children are no longer kids and they have taken on a life and journey of their own. This is the empty nest stage of Mom Guilt.

MOM 8: I had to learn how to see them as friends but also as my children. I want the best for them, but it's not my role to parent them anymore unless they ask for help.

MOM 9: I have four kids over the age of 25 and I feel more guilt now because of fear of loss. I only have limited time with them, and I need to make the moments we have together that much more special.

The spotlight is on you now. Imagine you are "Mom #10" in my interview process. Which Mom Guilt phase are you in right now? What is your most recent experience with Mom Guilt?

This is just a small sampling of the many interviews which came to the same conclusion. Mom Guilt is real. It is nothing to be ashamed of, and certainly nothing to be afraid of.

Think of it more like an initiation into motherhood—a rite of passage. Every mom is going to go through some form of guilt, especially in the first phase when being a mom is new and it's easy to feel like they "can't do this."

Every mom I interviewed had a story about the early stages of being a mom—or feeling like a terrible mother for one reason or another.

Their kid being dropped

Falling off the bed or the couch

Feeding them frozen foods or juice

Letting them watch TV

Working too much

Not being able to provide

Almost every mom interviewed said Christmas or other significant holidays were a big guilt moment for them. Trying to fulfill kids' wants and dreams and make the holiday magical was too much—almost preventing them from enjoying the holiday altogether.

The pressure moms put on themselves is one thing. Add to that the pressure from family and friends and the relentless mom-shaming from other mothers.

Believe it or not, mom-shaming is a real thing. It's when moms bully each other for their different parenting styles and choices. It's the battle between disposable or cotton diapers, breastfeeding or formula, public school or private school, and so on.

As if being a mom is not difficult enough, moms actually lay guilt trips on each other. It can be a bit much at times.

When I was in my dark place during the first year of being a mom, I wondered why I didn't hear more about Mom Guilt. Why did I feel like I was the only mom going through this monstrous guilt?

If I wanted to tell someone, I was afraid that they would assume that I was exaggerating and being emotionally sensitive and needy, so I didn't tell anyone. The irony of it all—I felt guilty about talking about my Mom Guilt.

I now see why I felt so isolated. I had no one to connect with emotionally because Mom Guilt felt taboo. No one was talking about how hard it was, especially that first year, and so I was on an emotional island all alone. I know now that I'm not the only one that went through that.

The good thing is that this book is the emotional rollercoaster emergency exit. If you're in that same dark place that I was, it's time to either get off the ride or invite all your favorite humans onto it to support you and join in on the conversation.

Mamas, taboo or not, we are talking about the one thing no one wants to confront—Mom Guilt. It's the real deal, and we are confronting it.

Okay, it's time for me to again make myself vulnerable by sharing a few of my blog posts (there are more at the back of the book and on my website). Many of you will relate to my stress and anxiety. The reason I do this is that these are my raw emotions during that time when I was overloaded with Mom Guilt. I hope that my vulnerability gives you the courage to open your heart and do the same. It's very healing.

Part Two | Personal Blogs

December 2018

Birth Announcement

I got my Christmas wish, but not exactly the way I wished it. The past 60+ hours have been the toughest of my life. Christmas night, we went to celebrate with the Russell family. Not long after getting home, we ended up at the ER because I thought my water had broken early. I was lucky we were there, though, because although my water didn't break, we were admitted due to pre-eclampsia, and they started inducing me at about 2 a.m. the morning after Christmas.

After hours of waiting on my body to be ready and almost two hours of pushing, at 2:03 p.m., our little princess arrived! The two of us had a rough time along the way, and towards the end, I wasn't sure how we were going to make it, but we did!

Once she came out, her poor head was squeezed so tight it was deformed and bruised, and she had a headache, so she wasn't feeling well. She was so exhausted she wasn't eating, and at about 10 p.m., she gave her mother the scare of a lifetime as I held her blue, lifeless-looking body in my arms, screaming for help.

The amazing nurses came to our rescue and were able to get her breathing and her color back, and they took her to the NICU, where she has spent the last few days hooked up to monitors with 24/7 supervision. They have done every test possible and narrowed it down to her just needing time to learn to multitask and breathe while she's eating.

The last few days have been stressful and exhausting on all levels. I have never been so scared in my life. The good news is she was released back to our room today, and we all get to go home tomorrow! We will still have some things to monitor, and she will take all the attention as she still has what we call "episodes," but we don't mind.

Kudos to all the moms out there. This is hard!!!! We are still not home, and it's been quite the week for us.

Brynlee Charline Russell
- ✓ Born: Dec 26th @ 2:03 p.m.
- ✓ 7lb 1oz 20 3/4 inches long

January 2019
The Unexpected

I am a planner, so I was prepared for a baby to arrive. I was prepared to lose sleep, prepared for those middle-of-the-night, every-few-hour-feedings, prepared to go through all the diapers, wipes, and creams, do all the laundry, and learn how to be a mom and run my business at the same time. I was prepared for the pain of labor and recovery.

I wasn't ready for what our parenthood reality has been like the last couple of weeks. I wasn't prepared to live in a 400 sq. ft. hospital room for weeks. I wasn't prepared to see my baby turn blue, lose weight, stop breathing, go through test after test, and be poked in both hands, both feet, and the scalp. I wasn't prepared to learn about my baby's pain face and hurt cry so early on. I wasn't prepared to help hold her down through the process to get done what we needed to do.

It's been a rollercoaster that never stops; some moments you blackout, some you feel excitement, relief, panic, worry, hurt, fear, but all in all, you feel love. This little human has made us whole when we thought we already were, and she's testing us while testing herself, and we are all passing with flying colors.

(Let me add to this we spent a total of 32 days in that 400-square-foot hospital room, and I never once left the hospital, and I only left her room twice. Once to get my hair done and feel something other than the lifeless human I felt inside. Then another day, I was encouraged by the nurse to go down and make a necklace to honor myself and what I had created. Both times I left that room, I felt Mom Guilt and now realize that is what held me captive in there all the other days. What if something happened while I was gone?

What if she can feel that I am not there, and she thinks I left her? How selfish of me to get my hair done while she is in there hooked to machines.)

Mamas, I know some of you have been there, and some might be there in the future. I hope my book helps you realize that taking care of YOU is taking care of THEM.

Pre-Mom vs Post-Mom

Before she arrived ...

I said I wouldn't get the epidural.

I'll do everything they told me in birthing and breastfeeding class.

No pics of labor allowed.

I don't wanna see anything below the waist.

Don't cut me.

After she was born ....

I said I wouldn't allow pacifiers.

No formula, breast milk only.

I wouldn't spoil.

I would let her "cry it out."

She would wear all the outfits we bought.

I'll use the wipe warmer.

I won't bite her nails for her.

I won't kiss her on the lips.

Let's just say I did the opposite of them all and have since thrown my parenting plan out the window like I did my birthing plan.

Once you're in the moment, what you said you would do doesn't matter. It's what you decide to physically do.

Yeah, our child is different with her health situation, so some of these decisions I didn't even get to make as her mother, but as a parent, nothing is wrong unless you are doing harm.

You do you, mamas, and don't worry about what others say. Get opinions but knowing what works for them won't always work for you and your baby. How could it, after all, because you aren't them.

Our job as mothers is to help these little ones survive, grow, and thrive, while making sure they feel loved and safe. Everything else is just extra BS we figure out along the way!!!

Let's empower other moms, not put them down just because they "don't do it as you do."

xoxo xoxo

2020

Through Her Eyes

Parent Perspective

I'm not sure what has gotten into our child, but the terrible twos are here. She is defiant and stubborn. She fought for over an hour before going to bed the last two nights, and I'm so exhausted.

She wouldn't sit still, wouldn't stop blabbing, didn't want her blanket, kept yelling and throwing a fit when I would give it to her, wouldn't lay her head down—she even tried to hit me at one point!

I wish she would just give me a break.

Toddler Perspective

I'm not sure what mom's problem is lately.

I have had all these new thoughts and feelings since my birthday that are so exhausting. The only time I get her to myself to explain how I feel is at bedtime.

I try to tell her all about my day and how hard it was because the teachers just don't understand me, and she just shoves a bottle in my mouth and tells me to shhh and go to sleep.

Sometimes she even begs me, almost in tears, to just close my eyes and sleep.

She says that she's had a long day, and I'm like, "me too, Mom, that's what I'm trying to tell you!"

Doesn't she know I already listened to so many people at school today that I just want to get to choose for myself, and right now, I choose to have this moment?

I don't want to lay my head down or have a blanket on me.

I said no to her four times, and she kept putting a blanket on me and laying me back down.

Then she got upset when I threw it off and swung at her, but I only did it because she wasn't listening to me before.

I wish she would just give me a break.

This was Brynlee and I the last few nights, and tonight my husband handled bedtime because I just couldn't.

I have struggled with letting her be independent and strong-willed while also trying to keep my sanity at the same time.

Although I'm always up for a challenge, I felt defeated, so I started researching and reading up on two-year-olds and their minds, feelings, growth, changes, and regressions.

By the time I was done, I wanted to barge in there and validate all feelings she had.

I wanted to hold her and give her the comfort she was longing for the two nights prior.

I wanted to listen to whatever story she told and tell her I understood how she felt and that I hoped tomorrow would be a better day for both of us.

They are small, but they are mighty, and they are human with real feelings and real needs.

Although they can't tell us exactly what they need, they (try to) show us in ways we don't understand, so everything's lost in translation.

Being a parent is the hardest, most confusing job I have ever had, and it didn't come with a guide or any "how to" procedures. So, I am just learning as I go.

Tonight, I learned how to make her feel "seen" and how to validate her feelings even when they seem ridiculous.

Honestly, at the end of the day, isn't that what we all wish for?

Thank you for reading my blogs!

You can find more on my website: TheMaskedPoet.org

Even though I didn't realize it at the time, blogging or keeping a journal is one of the few sacred tools for maintaining sanity as a mom. Since we have become so accustomed to keeping our emotions and guilt to ourselves, it's a healthy outlet for clearing our minds.

As you learn how to address your Mom Guilt through the solutions offered in this book, I encourage you to use your blog or journal on a regular basis to keep track of your progress. Make sure you write about all your wins and positive experiences. Accentuate the positive and learn from any downtime moments.

Part Three | 7-Steps to Finding Inner Strength & Peace

Chapter 3

Step One | Find Your Center

"There is no way to be a perfect mother,
but a million ways to be a good one."

—*Jill Churchill*

When I first became a mom, I constantly compared myself to others, and I struggled running a business and being a full-time mom. At one point, my husband even asked me:

"Well, how do other moms do it?"

Insert shame and Mom Guilt here!

The problem is that other moms were also struggling, but no one was talking about it. We were all under the spell of Mom Guilt taboo. Moms were to be seen but not to be heard. Well, I'm here to change that.

A big part of the struggle is that moms are always looking to find the proper balance in their lives. They are looking to balance taking care of their entire family, their kiddos, doing all the mom stuff, career, and hopefully getting exercise and sneaking in some relaxation. It takes a lot of mental and emotional juggling. Even the most together super-mom will eventually break down from the never-ending sorting of mixed priorities. An overemphasis on the need to be balanced is a sure formula for Mom Guilt.

What if I told you that trying to find balance is like looking for a needle in a haystack? The needle is there, but you will exhaust yourself trying to find it.

Life is not about balance. I know that sounds contrary to what so many of the mindset coaches and gurus are saying but hear me out.

In real day-to-day life, people who are successful at what they do are completely out of balance. They are focused, not balanced. This happens because you must give your full attention to the task at hand if you want to also give it your best. You can only focus on one thing at a time. That's how the mind works. Multi-tasking is not balanced. It is focusing on one thing at a time, quickly, and then going on to the next thing—quickly.

Instead of looking for balance, you want to learn how to be centered while being out of balance. For example, if you were to walk across a tightrope, you would be out of balance 90% of the time. However, if your mind is centered and focused, you can adjust for the swings and sways of your body. The way you stay centered is by focusing on a single fixed point in front of you and walking toward that point.

Your center is in your mind. If you were to focus on the rope, you would be doomed because the rope is always in motion and will keep you out of balance. Focusing on the rope is the equivalent of focusing on your problems.

It's the same with being a mom or doing anything else. You want to learn how to find your emotional center of gravity so that you are not swayed by the many gyrations of life. Your emotional center of gravity is the one emotion that you can easily connect with that makes you feel at peace and centered.

Prayer, meditation, singing, hiking, painting, playing music, and quiet walks, are all examples of how you can find your center.

Most people think of balance as something they want to achieve. However, balance is an effect of a healthy, focused mindset. It is not the cause. When you learn how to be internally centered, the feeling of balance will follow.

In the movie Titanic, when the ship began to sink, the eight-member band assembled and played music to help calm the distressed passengers. They played continuously as the ship plunged into the ocean—knowing that they were doomed. They knew how to find their center amidst all the chaos.

If you know you have a habit of getting overwhelmed and out of balance when you are taking care of your kids or any of your other responsibilities, then the trick is to develop pattern recognition. You want to learn to recognize the situations and behaviors that trigger you and throw you off. When you are aware of and recognize your triggers, it allows you to quickly adjust your focus and do something that makes you feel peaceful and centered so that you don't become overwhelmed. I call these micro-breaks.

A quick meditation, prayer, or breathing exercise will help you get centered. A few quick jokes can also go a long way to help you clear your mind. You just need to give yourself permission to stop, breathe, and do your micro-break.

Here's an extreme example of me getting out of balance and not yet knowing how to find my center.

After selling my company and spending a year at home with my daughter, I felt guilty about not making money, so I started another business and then found myself not spending enough time with my family (insert Mom Guilt again) or doing what I love to do. I was just hustling at a business to make money, but there was no sense of purpose or fulfillment. I was out of balance because I had to sacrifice my family and creative time for my career.

My solution to my feelings of guilt around money was to put all my energy into working and making money. If I had known how to find my center, I would have first established my personal and family priorities and then built a source of income around those priorities. Instead, I reacted to my guilt, and my solution made everything worse.

To combat these extreme out-of-balance situations, I came up with a way to find your center by leaning into your guilt and using it to your advantage. I call it "Three Enlightened Solutions."

Chapter 4

Three Enlightened Solutions

ONE: Take Emotional Inventory

TWO: Chunk It Down

THREE: Use Your Guilt

ONE: Take Emotional Inventory

To find your center, you first must recognize what throws you out of balance. It is all about course correcting. What are the emotions that trigger your feelings of Mom Guilt?

Here's a few to help you think this through:

- Worry
- Stress
- Fear
- Impatience
- Anxiety
- Overwhelm
- Anger
- Loneliness
- Resentment
- Grief
- Shock
- Jealousy
- Sadness
- Envy

Now, ask yourself the below questions to help you identify your emotional triggers.

What are your primary emotions?

What emotions do you feel most often?

What emotions trigger your feelings of Mom Guilt?

What people or situations trigger these emotions?

What beliefs trigger your emotions?

This comes back to pattern recognition. If you recognize your emotional triggers, you can prevent the downward spiral of feelings of Mom Guilt.

TWO: Chunk It Down

Instead of becoming easily overwhelmed by all your commitments and responsibilities, chunk it down into smaller tasks that you can manage easily.

Here's a few different examples.

CLEANING: It is a given that your house will never stay clean. Instead of doing a major cleaning all at once and losing a big part of your day, break your house down into different zones, and get into a daily rotation where you work on a different zone each day. I had to learn this the hard way as I am a little OCD. Add in a baby and, well, let's just say I spent more time following her to clean up the messes than I did enjoying watching her make them.

If it's possible, hire a housekeeper to do the heavy cleaning, and you do the lighter share. This was a stress-free treat for me every other month or once a month if I gave myself permission to hire out. Or, if you are more creative than me, make cleaning a fun, interactive game with your family.

WEIGHT LOSS: After having a baby, one of the hardest hurdles is getting your body back and finding the time to even try. It can be overwhelming to think about the total amount of weight you want to lose and all the effort it will require. Instead, chunk it down into weekly mini goals. What can you do this week that will bring you closer to your goal? If you consistently do mini goals each day and week, you will build the habit for achieving your bigger goal.

RELATIONSHIPS: If you want to improve your relationship with your kids, spouse, or significant other, what can you do differently each day that will make a difference? Do you need to forgive? Stop judging? Let go of anger? Release expectations? What can you give or do differently that would make you both feel better about each other?

You get the idea. All progress comes from small, incremental improvements. Take your bigger goal, or the problem you want to solve, and chunk it down into solvable morsels. Follow your intuition. You will know what to do.

THREE: Use Your Guilt

Up until now, guilt has been a stumbling block. We are accustomed to our guilt using us, but it's time to flip it around and start using guilt to force us to get focused. Use it to set boundaries. Use it to find and create your center.

Guilt can be an action motivator. When you feel guilt, don't freeze, and stay there. Tap into that pattern recognition. Take appropriate action. Make a change, even if it's small. Do what works best for you to get centered.

Remember, the guilt that comes from trying to stay balanced is exhausting. You will sacrifice every ounce of your strength to be there for others—at the expense of your own well-being.

Centered Not Balanced

Being overwhelmed, out of balance, or centered are emotional habits. Most behaviors and reactions are habitual patterns. Before anything changes, you have to get real with yourself and decide that you want to create a new pattern. It takes a conscious, intentional effort to pay attention to your patterns and then self-correct. It's a choice that only you can make for yourself.

No one likes to feel guilty or feel as though they have lost control of their time or their life. You already know that Mom Guilt and all the drama that comes with it is not working for you, so take a moment to answer these four questions:

What are the consequences if you do not learn how to recognize your patterns and find your center?

By not being centered, what is the impact on you? Your spouse? Other moms or women who look up to you?

What behaviors is your kid learning from you by you not being centered?

What would your life look like if you had a reliable strategy for getting centered and you were no longer controlled by circumstances?

These same questions were thrown at me when I was on the fence about whether I wanted to create new patterns and make changes that would truly transform my life. But then it occurred to me that when the cost of staying the same is greater than the cost of change, that is when we make moves, and I was ready to move.

I had to get real and answer the questions myself. Here's what I realized.

> ANSWER 1: If I did not learn how to recognize my patterns and find my center, I couldn't even bear to imagine the woman I would become.

> ANSWER 2: I would be staying in an empty place with a victim mentality and carrying all the Mom Guilt. I imagined the long-term impact it would have on my marriage and if I would be the cause of our downfall. I had not considered at the time that other moms would be looking up to me. I have since learned there is always someone watching and that I need to pay attention to the example I am setting by my choices.

> ANSWER 3: I had to process what my daughter learned from my behavior. I hadn't fully thought of how my not being centered would impact her. I was in survival mode and made sure she was physically cared for, but I didn't consider her mental state when I had not acknowledged my own.

> ANSWER 4: This question gave me the ability to envision a future where I was centered and able to lead my family how my heart and soul longed to. Then I made a choice.

If Mom Guilt were no longer an obstacle, and you had a vision for the life you want to create, would you take these questions seriously?

Going through and answering these just to check mark a box will not move you forward. You must want a real, meaningful improvement and you have to be so tired of living with Mom Guilt that you are willing to make a change.

The life you desire is on the other side of learning how to find your center. Get out of the self-defeating habit of trying to find balance and create a new version for yourself that leads to having a more fulfilled life.

How badly do you want it?

Chapter 5

Step Two | Keep Your Word

*"Mama was a stickler on keeping your word. That's helped me to make
the right decision in so many situations. Because of that, I also think
really hard before I make a decision because I know
I'm going to have to see it through."*

—Reba McEntire

Keeping your word and living with integrity is a big part of overcoming Mom Guilt. I never understood the depth of integrity until I went through a group coaching program that opened my eyes. I discovered that integrity is far more than just being honest. It is also about keeping your agreements—with yourself and others. However, the meaning of integrity seems to vary depending on who you ask. To avoid any confusion and to keep things simple, for me, integrity means keeping your word.

There are only two choices when it comes to integrity. You either keep your word, or you fall out of integrity, which is when you do not keep your word.

It's easy to keep your word and have integrity when things are easy and going smoothly in your life. The real test of integrity is when you are confronted with difficulties or challenges that would make it easy to fall out of integrity, but you choose to keep your word.

Keeping your word means keeping your agreements. Throughout our lives, we are constantly making agreements with ourselves and others. We say we are going to do something, and we either do it, or we don't. Some agreements are in writing, some verbal, and others are implied.

Examples of agreements:

Written: Buying a car and making a written agreement to pay for that car.

Verbal: making a verbal agreement to drop off lunch to a friend or showing up early to help set up a party.

Implied: Because you became a mother, you will care for and raise your child.

Keeping your word in all your daily agreements can be difficult at times, but that is when it matters the most. If you habitually break your agreements with yourself and others, then it becomes more difficult to set and achieve goals because, in the back of your mind, you see yourself as someone who breaks your agreements. Similarly, other people will not take you seriously or will see you as unreliable if you are aloof about doing what you say you are going to do.

How do you feel when you don't keep your word?

Examples of what I feel are:

- Untrustworthy
- Lazy
- Worthless
- Unreliable
- Pushover

How do you feel when you do keep your word?

Some examples of how I feel are:

- Capable
- Trustworthy
- Powerful
- Confident
- Reliable

We have a choice when we make an agreement with ourselves or others—to follow through or not—which means we are choosing the outcome of that situation. If we keep our word, we reinforce our image of being a person of integrity. If not, then we are reinforcing the image of being unreliable.

For moms, the struggle with integrity goes deep. One of the subtle consequences of living with Mom Guilt is knowing, on some level, that you are compromising your integrity—not by being dishonest with others, but with yourself.

Mom Guilt is the feeling of carrying the weight of everyone else's problems on your shoulders while pretending that everything is okay. But it's not okay. It's not okay to compromise the integrity of your health and happiness. That's why I wrote this book and why you are reading it. We both agree that it's time to hold ourselves to a higher standard of personal integrity.

I have always been a people-pleaser and agreed to anything and everything. I wasn't listening to my own wants and needs, and I wasn't keeping my agreements with myself. I was just doing for others and putting their needs before mine. Any agreements I made with others were done out of guilt, which built resentment because I never wanted to do it in the first place.

When we do not keep our word, we lose trust in ourselves, and then we start to carry guilt. I have found myself there many times when I say, "No snacks before dinner." Then, by the fifth yell from my toddler that she is hungry, I give her a snack. At that moment, I know I have lost, but it is easier to give in than it is to keep my word.

The other consequence is that I am teaching my toddler that she gets what she wants when she cries or has a fit. My weakness is shaping her personality. In a very subtle way, that type of giving-in teaches a kid to become emotionally weak—potentially leading to developing the habit of being a victim instead of learning patience, resilience, and being self-reliant.

Tell me that I'm not the only one that does that. If you are guilty of giving in, I will tell you to forgive yourself and move on. Pick a different battle and try again because the Mom Guilt you pick up from knowing you didn't stay in integrity with yourself is too big to carry. Stay strong. Don't give in to the crying, but if you do, forgive yourself quickly and move on.

Keeping your word is important, not just for the sake of the agreement and personal integrity, but because each time you justify breaking an agreement, you are developing a belief that you are a person who does not keep your word. At some point, your mental stack of broken promises becomes part of your identity—making it more difficult for you to commit to changes in beliefs and behaviors.

When you don't keep your word, you compromise your character. It's not worth it. If you don't believe you, why would anyone else believe you?

The group coaching program on integrity also taught me that, as you stretch and grow personally, you will not always be able to keep your word. When that happens, you acknowledge it, and you recommit. By doing so, you keep the trust and confidence in yourself. There will always be times when things just fall apart, and you can't keep your word, but those should be the exception, not the standard.

If you have a habit of showing up late to meetings or appointments, you are habitually breaking agreements. But, if you let them know in advance that you are running late, you are maintaining your integrity.

Developing the habit of keeping your time commitments is an easy way to begin re-establishing your personal integrity and developing a stronger, more resilient mind. You will be surprised how much this helps when it comes to overcoming Mom Guilt.

I know that I am keeping my word when I am being true to myself, true to who I am, and true to what I want. I have learned the importance of being intentional about doing things that align with my moral compass, that get me closer to where I want to be in this world and who I want to become.

There's something empowering about the honesty that comes with keeping your word and even acknowledging and recommitting when you're out of integrity. The self-respect you build leads to a level of confidence you could never imagine. Likewise, when you keep your word or accept responsibility for when you don't, people develop a higher level of respect for you.

When it comes to overcoming Mom Guilt, recommitting to a higher level of integrity is what helps you to regain your emotional strength and personal power. But first, you must stop playing the victim.

Chapter 6

Step Three |Stop Playing the Victim

"You must take personal responsibility. You cannot change the circumstances, the seasons, or the wind, but you can change yourself. That is something you have charge of."

—Jim Rohn

Let's talk about our victim complex.

You know what I'm talking about.

My problems and my guilt are everyone else's fault. They just don't understand what I am going through or who I am.

Feelings of Mom Guilt and being a victim feed off each other. Think about it. Mom Guilt comes from thinking we are not good enough or have not done enough for our kids. We always have a basket of excuses to justify our feelings. When we justify, we are blaming an outside influence for our choices.

Victims blame other people and situations for their problems. It's an easy and convenient escape because when you blame outside forces for things that happen, you don't have to accept responsibility for the outcome.

It's easy to feel guilt when you are a victim.

"I feel bad about what happened, but it's not my fault."

The mantra of a victim is:

"It's their fault."

"If my husband wasn't always so busy with work, I could have been a much better mom."

"There's just not enough time in the day to take care of my kids and all my other responsibilities."

I lived my entire life in a victim mindset and blamed others every time things did not go as I wanted or expected. I had no concept of personal responsibility.

It's crazy how easy and convenient it is to be a victim and blame anything and everything. The real benefit is that you do not have to learn anything new or grow as a person when you are a victim. You live safely in the comfort of your predictable cocoon—pointing fingers at everyone and everything except yourself.

The crazy thing is, Mom Guilt and being a victim is an addiction. Once you get everyone trained to give you love, attention, and affection every time you feel down, upset, unloved, or neglected, why would you ever want to break free from that pattern? You get all the attention without any of the responsibility or risk.

Here's the problem. Being a victim and keeping your word do not mix. If you are committed to overcoming your Mom Guilt and raising your standards, and keeping your word, that must include bailing on your victim addiction game that has kept you emotionally insulated and safe.

Having a victim mindset is not something to be afraid of or embarrassed about. It's a learned behavior, but it is something you want to get past because it is an emotional trap. You will never overcome your Mom Guilt if you are committed to remaining a victim.

Keep in mind that freeing yourself from being a perpetual victim does not mean that nothing hurtful happened to you. You cannot deny the past. It just means that you have chosen not to allow that painful experience to define who you are or to hold you back from your potential. I have been through a fair share of legit "victim" moments as a child, but I had to stop letting that define me.

How do you know if you are caught in a victim mindset? You easily blame others. Your happiness and personal worth are based on other people's opinions of you, and your self-esteem is wrapped up in the need to be validated by others.

How do you liberate yourself from the habit of being a victim? It takes forgiveness, personal responsibility, and ownership.

Forgiveness

For a lot of moms, forgiveness is a difficult step. When we feel like we have been neglected, abused, or traumatized, the thought of letting go of that pain can be scary. The thing is, you don't forgive for the benefit of the people who harmed you. You forgive so that you can let go of the weight that is holding you back. Forgiveness is a sign of strength, not weakness.

When you forgive, you are not pretending that nothing happened to you, nor do you forget about it. You are just making a pact with yourself to let go of the pain so that you can move on.

Personal Responsibility

There is nothing more liberating than accepting 100% responsibility for your life and being accountable to yourself.

Mamas, this is the core to overcoming Mom Guilt. No one wants to hear it but let's be real. Nothing in your life is going to improve if you do not accept 100% responsibility for who you are and everything that has happened to you. You may not be responsible for the actual events in your life, but you are 100% responsible for the meaning you give to each experience, how you respond, and the choices you make.

Being accountable to yourself means you are living with integrity and keeping your agreements. It is the most therapeutic act—especially for me. When I recognize that I am playing the victim, I slam on the brakes and switch to accepting ownership for my decisions and actions.

Ownership

This is an extension of personal responsibility. When you own something that you did or that happened to you, there is no blame or excuses. You are just being real and honest, and you accept responsibility. You own the outcome—because that is your choice.

Here's a simple example based on something that happened in my life that will highlight the difference between blaming, personal responsibility, and ownership.

BLAME-VICTIM

"Ugh, my alarm clock didn't go off, so I missed my workout.

PERSONAL RESPONSIBILITY

If I was truly serious about working out, I would have set up back-up alarms.

OWNERSHIP

I really don't want to get up at 5 a.m. on a Saturday morning to work out. I just want to sleep in for once.

Here's how this scenario played out in full in my life.

Yesterday morning I got a late start to my day because I straight up snoozed my alarm.

By the time I did my workout and came back inside, my three-year-old had already woken up and was playing with a red laser light. I had no idea where she found it.

My kid was sneaking around, so I took it and asked: "Where did you get this? Brynlee, where was this!?"

Like she was even going to tell me.

I started looking around the house for anything else that was out of place. I found a little tub of stuff one would usually have in a junk drawer. In the tub were pins for sewing—yes, an open box of pins—a lighter, and the list goes on.

Panic and Mom Guilt kick in, and then enters the blame game.

How did my husband sleep through this? It could have been bad, but luckily, the laser did not shine in her eye.

Palm to forehead moment.

I was clearly not centered at this moment and quickly had to stop and use my own tools.

Was I in integrity? No!

Let's start with the fact that I said I wanted to get up and workout, yet I slept in and got a late start to my day. That's why she was even awake already.

Am I accepting personal responsibility? No!

Well, clearly, it was my husband's fault, right?

I acted like the victim here, but was I really?

Nope, once I got real with myself, I acknowledged that I am very aware he is a deep sleeper, which is why I work out at 4 a.m. while they are still in bed.

I also didn't wake him and say: "Hey babe, I slept in, so I am just going out to the office, and you are on baby duty."

I didn't say that because I didn't want to admit I was late!

Then let's just add in that he didn't even know this junk drawer tub existed, and I was the one that put it within her reach.

It's so easy to fall into the trap of being a victim. For me, when I can call myself out on my victim-minded excuses, I feel very liberated because it means I am paying attention.

Chapter 7

Step Four | Fill Your Cup First

*"Putting yourself first is not selfish. Quite the opposite.
You must put your happiness and health first before
you can be of help to anyone else."*

—Simon Sinek

When you first became a mom, how many times were you told to put your child first?

Most moms put their child first out of intuition and the desire to be an amazing parent. On the surface, it makes sense. Isn't that the role of a mom—to care for their child?

The answer is yes and no.

Our culture equates motherhood with self-sacrifice. It's almost a rite of passage—to be the hero by losing yourself, dropping your dreams, and abandoning your duty to your own inner peace. This self-sacrifice feels great at first, but it slowly erodes your mental health because it demands that you forego your own self-care and well-being. This can lead to resentment and depression, and yes, Mom Guilt.

In the end, it is your child that suffers when you always put them first. You cannot give them your best if you are not making your own nourishment your priority. Your child can sense when you are happy, sad, joyful, stressed, or depressed. Whatever you are feeling, they are feeling.

Let me promise you that your child has nothing to lose and everything to gain by you choosing to put yourself first.

I spent the entire first year of motherhood putting myself last. I lived in sweats, a mom-bun, and hairy legs, yet my baby was dressed to the nines.

The best version of you will show up for your kid when you fill your cup first. This does not mean being irresponsible or neglectful. It means having a daily discipline that keeps you centered. By that I mean creating a morning routine that I call the Power Hour. In other words, it's YOU time!

Here's the simple version of how it works.

Without sacrificing anything else in your life, or asking others to fill in the gaps, give yourself one hour of YOU time each day by waking up one hour earlier. This is going to be your Power Hour for supercharging your day.

Chapter 8

Power Hour

*"You have to calendar time for yourself even if you have
no idea what you're going to do with it."*

—Susie Bright

How you start each day is one of the most important decisions you will make. It sets the tone of your energy and focus for the entire day.

The choices you make are the life you live. You wake up every day with the control to choose how you begin each day.

If you start your day happy and up-beat after a morning workout, prayer, meditation, inspirational reading, and reviewing your goals, you are most likely going to have a great day.

However, if you start your day off by immediately checking your text messages, email, social media, or other external distractions, your thoughts are going to hyper-link in all sorts of crazy directions and your day is going to get off to a much rougher start.

Power Hour is about creating morning rituals that get your day off to the best start possible so that you can accomplish the most and feel like you are on top of your game.

The Power Hour is broken into four segments which I call pillars. Each pillar represents a specific area of personal growth that will help you find your inner strength and peace.

Before I get into the mechanics of how the Power Hour works, I first want to give you permission to not follow the disciplines out of obligation. When I first learned about this strategy, I got very overwhelmed and froze because I had a lot of resistance from my old patterns and felt locked-in, which wasn't helpful for my growth.

Use this as a guide only. I am inviting you on a journey with me to find the best way to spend YOUR Power Hour and it won't happen in the first week. It is not the destination but the journey that makes the magic in the end worth the struggle.

That being said, read through this a few times and then find your perfect Power Hour routine. Maybe follow mine, first until you settle into your best practices. If all else fails, just show up!

Chapter 9

The Four Pillars of Power Hour

Passion and Purpose

Power (Self-Love/ Self-Care)

Positive Circle of Influence (POS COI)

Profit — Expand Your Income

For each pillar, you will do a 15-minute exercise that will help you build confidence and self-respect.

Each of the four pillars is the foundation of your day. Once you figure out what it looks like for you, it is essential to hit each pillar in some way every morning because they support each other. It's okay if you fall off here and there but try to get back on target as soon as you catch yourself falling off track.

Think of it like a four-legged barstool. If one leg breaks, you may be able to shift your weight to the other three for a while, but eventually it will tip.

ONE: Passion and Purpose

PASSION: This is what you love to do that gets you excited. It's something that comes easily and naturally that you can do without any effort.

PURPOSE: Using your passion to help others.

Finding my passion and purpose was hard for me when I first started my Power Hour because I was an atheist, and in my eyes, I had zero talent. I spent this part of my power hour alone in silence. It was the hardest thing I had ever done, but it brought me closer to who I am because it was the only time I could be alone with my thoughts without any outside influences.

This is simple, but it may not be easy. Spend up to 15 minutes doing something related to your passion and purpose. It could be reading, writing, singing, reviewing goal cards, prayer, meditation, painting, drawing, or just being in the moment figuring out your passion.

I use this time to focus on my faith because that is where I found my passion and courage to live in my purpose. I read the Bible and then journal as a tool to better understand what I have read and how I can apply it to my life. Spending this solitude time with Jesus helps to keep me at peace and centered. It eases my stress and calms my worries.

My true passion is my commitment to personal and spiritual growth and sharing my experiences with other moms so that they can discover the best version of themselves. Being vulnerable is what allows me to grow. It fills me up so much, and it is freeing to not hide in the shadows. Through writing, podcasts, social media, and speaking, I use my passion to fulfill my purpose of helping other moms.

What is your passion? Purpose?

What were you created for?

If it's bigger things than you are currently doing, I encourage you to pursue them without feeling any guilt. It's okay to enjoy doing what you love to do. You don't need anyone's permission to get started. You only need to make the decision to do so and then to take the first step.

If you aren't sure just yet, that is ok too! I didn't know my purpose or passion for thirty-three years and I have a feeling it will continue to evolve over time. Just pick something you enjoy doing, add it to your 15-minute Power Hour, and see where it goes. Switch things up until you find that connection.

God made my purpose very clear last year, and it gave me permission to just be ME.

TWO: Power (Self-Love/ Self-Care)

This pillar is focused on your health and what fuels your personal power. Even though it looks different for everyone, the outcome is the same: greater inner strength.

For 15 minutes, do whatever nourishes and energizes your body, mind, and spirit.

Move your body! This doesn't mean you have to start some crazy workout routine. Just get your adrenaline going and your endorphins released. Let me tell you, it is better than any cup of coffee you could drink, and I am a coffee snob.

It could be yoga, a walk, sit-ups, jumping jacks, maybe just stretching, or dancing. Whatever it is, move your body in some way and get your blood and oxygen flowing.

Stimulate your mind! Your mind wants to think, so give it something helpful to think about. Give your thoughts focus and direction. Read inspirational books or magazines. Write in your journal. I also love doing daily affirmations in front of the mirror.

Energize your spirit! Your spirit naturally wants peace and happiness, so do whatever fuels that feeling. Prayer, meditation, breathing exercises, and intentional laughter are great methods for peace and happiness. I use the "Insight Timer" app and listen to "Manifesting A Positive Day" since it is a great mood-setter.

You know what is best for nourishing yourself, so go ahead and do it. You just need to give yourself permission to love yourself first without generating Mom Guilt feelings.

I started with a small, easy workout just to move my body, then a few minutes of meditation and a couple of minutes focused on positive affirmations that build my confidence. The way you talk to yourself matters, so I highly recommend finding affirmations that get you fired up.

You are your own worst critic. When you live with Mom Guilt all the time and beat yourself up with words, those things you tell yourself start to become true. This is why self-care is very important. You must become your best friend through meaningful habits that help you get energized and centered.

When you find what works for you, you will want to do it consistently. I promise this will be one of your favorite parts of the day.

THREE: Positive Circle of Influence

This pillar is about initially taking inventory of the people in your life, the people you associate with, and cleaning up the friendships and relationships in your daily life. For many moms, this will be both a reality check and a game-changer. Once you have established your tribe of positive people, you will spend this time pouring into them.

One of the most important decisions you can make when overcoming Mom Guilt is evaluating the people you allow to be a part of your life. Intuitively, you already know this. Sometimes, your negative emotions come from the dysfunctional people in your life who don't treat you properly.

Initially, when you start during these 15 minutes, you will take a close look at and evaluate all your relationships and decide which ones are worth preserving or restoring and which need to be discarded. Your ultimate objective is to clean out the negativity and commit to ONLY building a positive circle of influence. I learned the meaning of this from Gretna Carey at Zac's Ridge, and she referred to it as "POS-COI."

This can be tricky because some of the people you may want to distance yourself from could be close friends or family— maybe even your spouse or partner. When it comes to clearing out the negativity from people close to you, this can be a very delicate situation. Make sure you seek professional help so that you transition with the least amount of resistance and in a manner that is mutually beneficial.

You also want to use this time to evaluate how you are showing up in other people's lives. Don't complain about other people's negativity or lack of integrity if you are doing the same thing.

My writing coach, David Strauss, wrote a book that addresses this topic of cleaning up your negative relationships. It's called *Dancing with Vampires*. I suggest reading it right away.

In the book, he makes the point that if you are hanging around people who put you down and exhaust you mentally and emotionally, they are Energy Vampires. If you are a negative person and only see the bad in life, you might be your own Energy Vampire.

When I first read David's book, I realized I was a vampire, and then I also realized I was attracting other vampires to me and accepting their toxicity because it matched my own. That realization changed my attitude because I finally understood that you attract what you are, not who you want to be.

When it comes to Energy Vampires, limit their access to you because they are toxic and will tear you down without you even knowing it.

Most importantly, as you clear out the negativity, make sure you are replacing that space with new, positive, uplifting people. Your entire focus should be to create a positive circle of influence.

I learned a very powerful analogy about life from one of my life coaches, Gretna, who ran a three-day camp for personal growth and development called "Zac's Ridge" in memory of her son. She taught us to imagine your life to be like a garden. If there were weeds growing in your garden, wouldn't you pull them before they destroyed your flowers?

Negative people are the weeds in the garden of your life, and you must pull them before they take over. Gretna has since passed away. My daughter is named after her as she changed my life for the better.

Take a moment to think of the main people in your life. Not just family, but all the people who are a part of your daily flow: in your home, at your place of work, other moms you hang around, your family, etc. Are they negative or positive?

Your garden is meant to flourish, full of color and light. Don't sacrifice it for some weeds. Do some clean-up, mamas.

Once you have established who fits into your positive circle of influence, then use these 15 minutes on the ones who support you, pour into you, speak life into you, shine a light on your dark days, and encourage you. For me, this looks like journaling and texting.

I write whatever is on my heart. First, a journal entry for myself is usually just my thoughts and emotions at that moment. It could be a letter to my bestie, Trinity (what I call God), or reaching out for guidance for something I am struggling with. Then, a letter to my husband and one to my daughter, Brynlee. It usually talks about what she did the day before, things she's saying or doing that I want to remember, and my feelings at the time.

In addition to my journaling, I send Good Morning texts to my best friends and my mom and dad. Sometimes it's long, and sometimes it's just an "I love and miss you."

FOUR: Profit — Expand Your Income

This is the pillar for your financial health. Just as you need to take care of your body, mind, and spirit, you also need to be financially responsible.

My first year as a mother was stressful and lonely. I was in survival mode. Drinking and spending were my outlets. At the end of the year, my husband and I looked at our finances. We saw that I had spent $3,000 on baby bows. Yes, bows that she grew out of so fast that I was literally throwing money away. We laugh about it now, but ladies, shopping therapy is a real thing, and I had to acknowledge that and take responsibility. (I won't even mention the Starbucks total.)

When you first start this pillar, dedicate your 15 minutes toward evaluating how you are spending your money and if your current income situation is going to realistically keep you going. If you are enrolled in shopping therapy like I was, this would be a good time to look more closely at that and quit the habit because it is not a healthy way to find love and connection with yourself and is masking your need for personal growth.

This is also a good time to evaluate your source of income. If you are not the primary income earner in your family, what would your situation look like if there was a medical emergency or death, and you lost your source of income? Are you prepared for that? Do you have the proper insurance policies in place? This is critical because if you don't address these, you are setting yourself up for some major Mom Guilt if you can't support your kids financially.

Mamas, take money seriously. I have always had a love/hate relationship with money because of childhood financial situations. Sadly, we need it to live, and it affects every part of your life and your kids' life. It affects education, health care, food quality, lifestyle, the neighborhood you live in, the car you drive, plus every other part of life.

Once you have your finances in order, start to use these 15 minutes to learn something new that can become a source of income for you—something you love and enjoy. You also want to spend time learning and improving in your current career if you have one.

If you do not want to work and truly just want to be home with your kids, and you can make that happen, then use these 15 minutes to research ways you can help them learn and grow so that they can become successful adults.

I have spoken to many stay-at-home moms, and their biggest guilt is around not being able to help support the family financially. That was a big problem for me, too.

During my first year of being a mom, overspending was my therapy of choice. I'm sure I'm not the only one who has tried to spend their way to happiness. The second year of my daughter's life, I was at home due to the COVID economic shutdown.

I remember feeling overwhelmed because, although it was nice to have that time with her, I felt as though I should have been bringing home a paycheck. I felt guilty for even the smallest purchases, like a cup of coffee or anything at all. I felt like my freedom had almost been given up by choosing to be a stay-at-home mom.

Can you relate?

To address the guilt and make myself feel worthy, I found ways to earn money by working from home. I made clothing for a while and became a market partner for Monat (I am still a shampoo dealer and swear by their products). I got my life insurance license and helped protect families like mine. The training I received in insurance taught me the importance of having my financial structures in order.

Plan for the best. Prepare for the worst.

At first, I was trying to find a way to contribute out of guilt. I just wanted to be a mom and somehow earn an income doing just that—which sounds silly at first, but many of you can relate, but when I embraced my guilt and did something about it, a whole new world of opportunity opened for me.

Let me tell you, mamas, if there was ever a time to be able to work from home and be a mom, it is now. The way the world has moved to virtual careers has given us our liberty and power, so make sure you capitalize on it!

After going through a Passion-to-Profit coaching program with Sabastian Sang Huynh, I discovered my voice and my passion for wanting to help other moms. Then, an insurance colleague introduced me to my writing coach, David Strauss, and the next big step was using my story and message in this book to inspire moms all over the world through speaking and being an influencer.

With this new sense of passion, I am using my 15 minutes of Profit in my morning Power Hour to learn something new that will help me build upon my passion as a coach, writer, and social media influencer to reach more moms and have a more significant impact.

I watch YouTube motivational videos. I read posts in other mom groups so that I can learn about the struggles moms go through and how I can help. I go through coaching programs to become a better leader, and I stay curious in all I do.

Are you making money doing what you love to do?

If not, what is getting in your way?

Have you even looked into it yet?

What do you love doing that, if you could find a way to make money doing it from home, you would get excited? Even if you can't yet picture yourself making money doing something you love, do some research, and explore some options.

Maybe you will be like me. I met my writing coach through my work selling insurance, which led me to reading his book, *Dancing with Vampires*, and now here I am, turning my Mom Guilt problem into my power.

It may sound crazy, but if you lean into your problems and face them, that is where you find your purpose and potentially your financial power, too. That's why this Power Hour is so important. You must create the right environment for yourself to learn and grow. You have to get out of your comfort zone and give yourself new challenges. Growth never happens when you are stuck doing what is safe or comfortable. You must stretch your mind and your beliefs.

Your Power Hour is not something you do just when you are home. Instead, it becomes part of your everyday life. For example, if you are on vacation or traveling away from home, preplan for what your hour will look like and adjust your plans to keep your agreement with yourself.

Chapter 10

Putting it All Together

The Power Hour is like a four-legged stool. Each of the four segments are designed to work together. If you remove one of the legs, it gets very wobbly because the other three legs can't make up for the one that is missing.

Your very first Power Hour will be your brain-storming session. During that time, you are going to think about each of the pillars and come up with a strategy for moving forward.

Summary — The Four Pillars of Power Hour

Passion and Purpose

What are you passionate about? What is your purpose?

Power (Self-Love/ Self-Care)

What can you do each day to begin your journey of self-care?

Positive Circle of Influence

Take inventory of the people in your life. Where do they fit in? Are they giving you positive energy or are they negative and dragging you down? Pour into those who pour into you.

Profit – Expand your income

What new sources of income can you bring into your life that will align with your passion and purpose and empower you as a mom?

Take the Power Hour seriously. It may be difficult at first, but that's normal. It's never easy to start a new habit, but it's always worth it.

Chapter 11

Step Five | It Takes a Village

"As moms, we are in it together—raising the future.
We are a tribe of future makers.
So, let's support each other."

—Marissa Hermer

Mamas, don't fool yourself. You can't do this on your own. It takes a village to raise a child.

If you genuinely want to be the best mom possible, without all the guilt, it is a must that you build a support team of people you know and trust. Different people play different roles. No one person can be everything for you.

When my husband and I first met, I fell madly in love and swore I only needed him, just him, forever and ever. So, I packed up my life and moved away from everything and everyone I had ever known.

I lived with him in Texas and struggled to keep up with my family relationships long distance, especially as a new mom. After four years and through the isolation of the pandemic, I decided to move back home to Arizona. My husband, daughter, and I now live on our family farm, and I am living with and amongst my positive circle of influence—learning about agriculture. All I can say is that the sooner you accept that no one person can be all people for you, the sooner you will find your positive, supportive tribe.

I remember from a young age hearing, "Don't take financial advice from broke friends." This advice applies in all areas of life.

I went through another coaching class with Stephen LaDuque and Jill Wade, where they taught about having different "tables" in our life. Each table is an analogy for an important part of our life. We can have spiritual tables, mental, social, or financial tables, or whatever other area that is important to us. I learned that not everyone can sit at my spiritual table (i.e., my prior atheist self).

When I first did that process with them, my husband was only allowed to sit at my financial table. He has since been invited to others.

The idea of tables made me realize that it really does take a village to live a healthy life. Your village needs to consist of at least six teams to make things work and flow with the greatest ease.

Here's a breakdown of those six teams:

Social Team

These are your fun people, but not the ones you go to for advice or support. You know who they are, the ones you call when you need a mommy night out.

Support Team

These are the people who are mentally and emotionally mature and can guide you from experience. They are there when you need them.

Financial Team

These can be people you know and trust; however, I also suggest looking into a professional financial coach who can help you get everything in order without profiting long- term from your gains.

Mindset Team

These are the people who will challenge you to learn and grow. They are other successful moms, entrepreneurs, coaches, and mentors.

Spiritual Team

If you are on a spiritual path, no matter what you believe, these are the people who will help you grow spiritually. Not just religious leaders, but also people who have a healthy insight into how to live a life of integrity with values and morals. They will help you make good decisions during difficult times.

Wellness Team

Taking care of your mind and body is non-negotiable. To make this happen, you want to identify the people who can guide and influence your physical and mental health. This can include a personal trainer, chiropractor, acupuncturist, massage therapist, or anyone else that you feel can help you keep your mind and body running at peak performance.

Those are my six recommendations

The point is, make sure you create teams in the areas of your life that matter the most.

If you have developed a habit of being fiercely independent, I challenge you to lean on your people and watch them stand in their power and help you.

Everyone needs a support team. I used to think I had to do it all and be all things for everyone, but that's just not possible. It's stressful and leads to Mom Guilt.

I used to think my husband could read my mind or at least understand what I was thinking and feeling. Does anyone else feel that way? Once I realized I just needed to show him how to help and make requests, he would rise to the occasion every time. He even mentioned feeling better about himself because I needed him or asked for his help instead of just doing it all myself.

I can also remember all the people who offered to help in so many ways when I first had my daughter. I turned them all down because I thought I was supposed to do this all alone. Why not? I was the mother, after all.

If I ever have another child, I will plan ahead and build my team in advance.

Have you built your team yet? If not, here's what you need to do to begin right now.

After you identify the teams you need in your life, make a list of anyone who has offered to help you with your mom duties that you previously turned down, and contact them.

Who can you reach out to that you trust—that cares about you and supports you?

Work from that list until you have your teams in place.

Don't hesitate. Start now.

Now that you understand the Power Hour, are you ready to take a challenge…?

In the next chapter, I am going to invite you to join *The Mom Guilt Movement* by first taking the Mom Guilt Challenge, which will help put you back in the driver's seat of your life. Even though we covered a lot of different ideas in this book, the challenge will focus on the four pillars of the Power Hour.

The goal of the challenge is for you to begin creating healthy daily habits that strengthen your mind, body, and spirit so that you feel like you are in control of your life rather than being pulled apart by the demands of being a mom.

The benefit of taking this challenge is that it will give you permission to make your life your priority so that you can be fully present for your child.

Are you ready to step into the challenge and rewrite the script of your life?

Let's go!

THE MOM GUILT

MOVEMENT

Chapter 12

Step Six | Join the Challenge

"If you really care about starting a movement, have the courage to follow and show others how to follow. And when you find a lone nut doing something great, have the guts to be the first one to stand up and join in.
— *Derek Sivers*

The **Mom Guilt Movement** is an army of moms who have committed to improving their lives and supporting each other while participating in the **Mom Guilt Challenge.**

Okay, mamas, let the fun begin. It's time to let your hair down, put on your sweatpants or yoga pants, and take the first step toward breaking the habit of Mom Guilt. It's time to find your inner strength and peace.

This is a self-guided personal challenge. Since there are so many different moms and personalities taking this challenge, I'm going to share the most direct path to getting the fastest results, but by all means, do this at your own pace. You know what is best for you.

I call this a challenge because it will push you outside of your comfort zone. It's not easy to break old habits and start new ones, so be easy on yourself when you first get started. This is not about perfection but about bettering your best each day.

Now, in preparation for the first step, re-read chapter 9. Focus on the Power Hour and its four main pillars so that you can refresh your mind about the content.

After you've done that, come back here for the next steps.

Step One — Acknowledge

Acknowledge to yourself that Mom Guilt is a problem for you and that you want to find your inner strength and peace.

Take inventory of all the situations that trigger your feelings of Mom Guilt.

Step Two — Make the Commitment

Find some time, any time of day, and think about the Four Pillars in relation to your life. How do they fit into your current approach to life?

- Do you have a passion and purpose?

- Are you currently engaged in any form of regular self-care?

- Can you identify the people (if any) in your positive circle of influence?

- What are you doing for income? Do you enjoy it? Do you want to find something more rewarding or fulfilling?

After you think those ideas through, decide which day you are going begin your Power Hour, and commit to it.

Step Three — Be Intentional

Be intentional about giving yourself an extra hour first thing in the morning to focus on the Four Pillars of your Power Hour. Remember, the reason you do this first thing in the morning is to start your day with small wins that give you strength and peace of mind.

Part of being intentional is being honest with yourself about the many excuses that could hold you back from making the commitment and following through. Make a list of your best excuses so that you recognize them when they pop in your mind.

Do not compromise the timing of this. Do not wait until after the kids are off to school or at night before bed. If you do that, you are missing the entire point—which is to fill your cup first before you give any time or energy to anyone else.

Step Four — Be Consistent

This challenge is about consistency. Pick a target for how many consistent days you want to do the Power Hour and then do your best to keep that commitment. I recommend ten days in a row.

If you miss a day, don't get down on yourself. Take some time to think about the habit or excuses that got you distracted, start again the next day, and keep your eyes on that consistency target.

Keep doing this until you hit your consistency goal. The most difficult part of this challenge is the consistency. Once you get it, you will fall in love with the new you.

Step Five — Celebrate

After you complete your first consistency target, celebrate your victory by buying yourself a bouquet of flowers, a mani-pedi, or some other fun way to celebrate. Then post on the Facebook group so we can all celebrate with you!

Step Six — Stretch Your Goal

After you celebrate, repeat the challenge, but this time extend your goal by adding more days to your target. If you did ten days the first time, go for 12-15 days the next time.

If you're feeling frisky and want to double down on the challenge, try this Supermom Bonus. Each time you goof up, start over again from zero until you can hit your target consistently.

Step Seven — Journal

At the end of each day, keep a written journal of your accomplishments and personal breakthroughs. Include your feelings, good or bad, and any resistance that you felt from your old habits and beliefs. This is your opportunity to be honest with yourself so that you can develop inner strength and resilience.

Join The Challenge

Facebook:
Request to join the Facebook Group:
'The Mom Guilt Movement' > Go to: "Featured"

Or...

TheMaskedPoet.org
- ✓ Choose "The Mom Guilt Movement" at the top
- ✓ Click to download, and then read the four tools
  1. The Challenge Guide
  2. Power Hour Summary
  3. Daily Power Hour Journal
  4. Progress Tracker

Mom Guilt Challenge Guide

Download from two locations:
1. Facebook Group under "Featured"
2. TheMaskedPoet.org
   — Click "The Mom Guilt Challenge" at the top and then download the worksheets

Chapter 13

Step Seven | Invite a Friend

"I alone cannot change the world,
but I can cast a stone across the waters
to create many ripples."

—*Mother Teresa*

Mamas, this is the best part of the seven steps. This is where you get to shine and help others.

Overcoming Mom Guilt and the Mom Guilt Movement are about building a community of moms who want to support each other to be their best for themselves and their families.

The world needs more emotionally healthy and strong moms. Other moms need to see that they are not alone and that there is a tribe of women who have been in their shoes—ready to lead them to find their inner strength and peace.

It's time for us to step out of our past, our lingering guilt, and our shame, and step into our power.

Invite a friend to read this book, take the challenge, and join the Mom Guilt Movement.

We can do this—together.

Chapter 14

Epilogue

*"It's time for us to do more than just survive,
we were made to thrive."*

—*Casting Crowns*

You did it! Thank you for finishing this book and having the courage to confront your Mom Guilt. All the ideas I mentioned in this book have worked for me, and they can work for you, too.

Reading this book is your first step in joining the **Mom Guilt Movement** and the first big leap toward learning how to find your inner strength and peace.

When I applied the ideas in this book into my life, there were three that stood out as being a significant part of overcoming my Mom Guilt and finding my center.

- ✓ Keeping your word and being accountable to yourself for your life.
- ✓ Starting your day with the Power Hour and filling your cup first in the morning is essential in your journey.
- ✓ The icing on the cake is developing a tribe of other moms whom you can inspire and encourage and who can help you on the days you struggle.

The ideas that stand out the most for you are the areas where you need to grow the most.

Everyone is going to have their unique experience from this book, but I know for sure that once you join the movement, a whole new life is going to begin to open for you. It's not going to happen overnight, and you may find some resistance from your old habits and maybe even from the people in your day-to-day life, but it will be worth it.

Remember, you are your own person. It is your life. You are responsible for your choices and the environment you create for yourself, your kiddos, and your family.

Being happy, finding inner strength and peace, and having a sense of purpose are essential for your overall well-being. You can live and enjoy your own life while still being the best mom you can be.

Let's Connect on Social Media

Join the Facebook group

"The Mom Guilt Movement"

Please join our growing global community of moms who are taking back their life and reclaiming their happiness and sense of purpose.

This Facebook group will help you connect with other moms just like yourself so that you can find a supportive tribe outside of your home.

Accountability, support, understanding, forgiveness, and grace are a few of the benefits from being a part of this group.

Follow on Instagram

@The_Masked_Poet_

Blog

TheMaskedPoet.org
- ✓ Subscribe to the blog and email list
- ✓ Link to my YouTube and podcast

Acknowledgements

I would love to take a moment to thank the many people that have played a role in this book coming to life.

In no particular order but with all the gratitude I have in me:

Huge THANK YOU to my writing coach David Strauss. When we started this process, it looked totally different, but you let me have a voice and supported me through all my changes, and helped my ideas come to life. I am forever grateful for you and look forward to writing together more!

A huge thank you to my mother, Amy Holmes, for always being such a great role model mother to me and for all the support and encouragement to use my voice and help others. You have always been my best friend, and I hope to fill your shoes someday for

Brynlee. Love you more…

All the love and appreciation for my daddy, Joel Holmes. You have always been my biggest fan and hype man when I need it. Thank you for your honesty and wisdom through the years that helped me be vulnerable while writing this book. You will always be my Hero.

To my husband, Bryan Russell, thank you for believing in me and my vision for this book and movement. Thank you for the late-night and early morning editing help and for encouraging me to be me through the whole thing. Thank you for always supporting my dreams. I love you for everything you are and everything you are not.

My baby girl Brynlee, thank you so much for making me a mama. You have no idea how long I waited for you. I love your gypsy spirit, your kind soul, and how big you love. Without you, this book would not exist, and I would not be able to help other mamas feel seen and heard. Keep challenging the world, stay curious and never apologize for being YOU. I love you, Charlie.

To my daughter, Brooklyn, you made me a mom when I thought all hope was lost. You have given me the gift of chosen love and you make it so easy. I am so proud of the woman you are becoming, and I am grateful Brynlee has a big sister role model like you.

I appreciate you, Christina Wright. You were my first chosen child that gave me a sense of what parenting felt like—to love someone else more than you love yourself. I am so grateful that we are best friends now, and I thank you for always being my lifeline. Love you to the moon and back.

To the girl that stole my heart at 4 months old. Thank you, Lexi, for showing me what unconditional love looks like. You showed up at a time when I didn't even know I needed you. You were such a blessing to me. I hope someday you see yourself through my eyes and know just how amazing you are. Olive Juice.

To my best friends, Larry & Kristi King, thank you for being the constant genuine people in my life. I am so grateful to have your family as role models for my family. Thank you for loving my family like your own. You guys are irreplaceable. I love you—to infinity and beyond!

Sabastian Huynh, you were the first person in a very long time that saw how powerful I was and refused to let me hide. You forced me to be raw and honest with myself and taught me so much. This book was born from your coaching. You saw me, and then you helped me see myself—what the Christmas! Thank you from the bottom of my heart!

So much of who I am today and the mother I can be is thanks to the late Gretna Carey, who coached me through my past. You welcomed me with open arms from day one, and you never gave up on me, even when I gave up on myself. Thank you! I love and miss you.

Yashmeri Kuilan, you have been such a great friend through all of this and have always shown me so much support and encouragement. Love you, girl!

To Bonnie Jo Popovich and Amanda Atwood, you ladies have inspired me since I met you. Before I became a mom, I remember taking notes as I heard about your parenting style because I saw it always came from a place of love. Bonnie, your support through the whole process to get to this place is unmeasurable. You have been the best friend and support system to me, and this book wouldn't exist without you. Thank you! Love you, girls!

I don't even know where to start with you, Misty Vaughan. Thank you for praying for me even when I couldn't pray for myself. Thank you for all your guidance through the last year while I wrote this book. I love and appreciate you more than you will ever know.

My heart, sister Melissa Hale Houston, your words of wisdom get me through the hard times. While writing this book, I often heard you in my head cheering me on and reminding me how wonderful I was when I had forgotten. I am so thankful to have you in my life. Love you.

Debbie Hebert, thank you so much for always encouraging me to do and say what is on my heart. For seeing the good in me and knowing I would always find my way. You are an inspiration to me. Love you, sis.

Thank you to my mother-in-law, B.J. Mitchell West, for helping me through the rough first year as a mother. You were always eager and willing to do anything to help. I survived the first few months by your grace. I love you!

A big thanks to my father-in-law (aka Papa) Paul Russell for many nights and weekends entertaining my toddler Brynlee while I wrote this book. You have been such a huge support system, and we want you to know it never went unnoticed.

Your girls love you.

Thank You for Believing in Me!

Speaking of POS COI (positive circle of influence), these people have been my biggest supporters through this journey, and they are a big reason that this book exists.

Thank you for believing in me and my purpose!

Yashmeri & Luis Kuilan

Corey & Bryanna Cox

Thao & Danny Nguyen – artist

Jeanne Lewis

David Paul Russell

Amy & Joel Holmes

Phil & Mindy Hatch

David & Melissa Houston

Medicare Misty

Tandra Blair

Barbara Scheele

Misty Bolt

Steven LaDuque and Jill Wade

Misty Bolt's Mom Guilt Story

When did my Mom Guilt begin?

It all started after having a child out of wedlock. I did not have the time to do the proper planning to organize and put together the family support that a child needs when brought into the world. Doing it on my own without any support for the first six years was tough. Every day I had to drop him off at daycare at 7 am each morning and was the last parent to pick up their child at night. It was frustrating for him and me because I was still working when I picked him up and could not give him the attention he deserved.

The first daycare I found was somebody that worked from home. I really couldn't afford daycare, so it was the least expensive option that I could find. On the seventh day of daycare, I got an urgent call to pick up Landon because of an unforeseen emergency affecting the babysitter's husband.

Out of respect for privacy, I will not go into details, but the effect was me feeling shame, embarrassment, and guilt—and for good reason. We're the parents. We are supposed to keep our children safe, and it's our job to mentor them. It's our duty as parents to provide safety, security, and a stable living, and when something happens to us, we cannot always be that person.

I was raised by two teenage parents, so I didn't have a lot of guidance because they were still young and inexperienced. But I did learn a lot about what not to do. Sometimes I got angry because Landon wanted my attention, but I had ten million things to do on top of trying to take care of him, running my life, spending time with friends, and dating. It's like the Mom Guilt never, ever stops. No matter how hard I tried to do my best, there was always something that came up to pull me in different directions.

Before Landon was born, I had a friend that wanted to be my Lamaze coach. He insisted that I need to go to Lamaze to learn how to have a safe and healthy pregnancy and birth. He had liked me for a long time in college, but I just wasn't interested—really in anybody. I think I was interested in surviving. I was in survival mode or just fun mode. And so, he became my Lamaze partner, and we ended up dating each other. On the day Landon was born, he decided it was too much for him, so he left that day in the hospital just before he was born. The Mom Guilt from that was rough. I remember thinking to myself, "I can't even find someone to help with the birth, let alone have a family to support."

Lack of money is a big part of mom guilt. It was very frustrating for Landon and me when I didn't have money for his birthday or to take him on a trip or go on his school field trips. It was always so exhausting. It was even more frustrating when I couldn't help him with his homework because I was not smart enough. Landon was in private school, so some of the stuff they were doing was tough.

I was raised in an inner-city school before they decided that other kids needed to go to a different school zone to be around smarter kids. You know, I always felt guilty when I had to say, I didn't have the money, I'm sorry, I can't afford that. He used to say, Mom, just use your credit card, or mom, just write a check.

I tried to explain to him that there's got to be money behind that. You can't just write a check and use your credit card. You know, one day, I was so stressed out that he became stressed out. I remember one day he got sick and was just throwing up all the time, and I said to him, can't you just not throw up? You know, ever again? And he said, I'm sick, I'm helpless. I felt a lot of guilt for making him feel that way when he was already sick.

You know, I live with that today. He's about to be 21. When I look back, I wonder, Did I do enough? I didn't always make the right choices, but I tried. I tried hard to do my best. And I sacrificed a lot. But the question always comes up in my mind, did I sacrifice enough?

He always used to tell me that he wanted a brother, which is why my place was where all his friends would hang out. And I remember saying, you know, it's not up to me about having another one, and I wasn't going to have one out of wedlock again—or even single because it's not fair to the child, and it's not fair to the parent.

One time I was dating somebody, and he was the total wrong person for us. I was trying to fit a square peg in a round hole and make this family. And when he left, I said to my son, you know, this was your fault, but it wasn't. I remember the next day coming in and reiterating that it is not his fault. Nothing is your fault. I mean, of course, he's going to do some things wrong, but when it comes to those kinds of things, it's not his responsibility.

Being a mom—especially a single mom—is a hard job. I think it's one of the hardest jobs that we can do if we do it right. I think it's even harder when you do it wrong because then you live with the guilt of trying to make up for your mistakes.

Now looking back at him at 21, I wish I had done more. I sell Medicare and have for sixteen years. I've been with a lot of seniors, and they would tell me—you know, it goes by fast. And I remember thinking, does it? But it does. It just doesn't seem like it.

At the time I was raising him, I was only making $1,100 per month. Of that, $500 was rent, and another $500 was daycare, which is why I was always so broke. My mom was going to help me, but she was still young, still in her partying mood. Half the time, she wouldn't show up.

When I think about my mom, nothing really bothered her about the way she raised us. She never took responsibility for what she did. The good thing is, I can say to this day that I have a fine man. He's 21, so he's making 20-year-old mistakes. He didn't finish school, but he had two opportunities to take over his dad's business or my business. The guilt sets in. Did I push him enough? Did I push him too much? Why is he not wanting to go to school? He didn't take his basketball scholarship.

I know we have to let our kids make those kinds of mistakes. But we love them dearly. I think the best advice I got was from her husband, which his dad gave him. He said, I gave you eighteen years of guidance and freedom. And now it's time for you to use those tools. And then what you decide to do with them is on you. And I think that's the best advice any parent could give who is still here. But I was still constantly, you know, bailing them out.

So parenting is not for the faint of heart. It's not an easy job. I think I worried more than I ever worried before, but it's more love than you could ever imagine—unconditional love—especially for a mom and a boy.

Thank you for your time.

I hope this helps some of you put that aside and realize that you're doing the best that you can. Open communication with other moms and other groups is the best thing. I think this book is the greatest idea ever. Thank you for putting it together.

You're amazing, and I'm glad that God introduced us; and I wish all the moms the best.

And I say lay down the guilt and pick up the wine.

Hope you have a great day.

Thanks!

Misty Bolt, Tennessee

Family LEGACY 95

FAMILY LEGACY 95

Family LEGACY95 & Fathers Legacy is a non-profit organization created to support families in the creation of a healthy, happy, hardworking legacy of love.

FL95 was created in 2018 by Drs. Jill Wade & Stephen LaDuque in honor of their journey as single parents & now a blended family. This organization is committed to helping busy families create a greater connection, communicate in a more healthy and grounded way, and experience fun in natural surroundings at their 115-acre 4th generation cattle ranch outside of Stephenville, Texas.

They also offer one-on-one & group coaching & utilize their custom app called Progressive Legacy daily in their coaching programs.

For more information:

254-592-1767

Fathers-legacy.com

Stephen@Fathers-Legacy.com

A Few More Blogs

June 2021

Baptism and Testimony

At a young age, I had a negative experience at church, lost my faith in God, and never looked back. I was, by definition, an atheist until November 2020.

Growing up as young as 12, I can remember telling my mom my purpose in life was to overpopulate it with my babies.

In my twenties, I decided to chase my dream of becoming a mom, but without fail, I kept falling short.

I was told by doctors of some medical issues and that I would probably never get pregnant, but the chances of it happening would be better the sooner I tried. So, I tried with a vengeance because I knew that was my purpose in life. I beat myself up every month that I couldn't succeed at the one thing I felt I was put on this earth to do.

I got into a bad place and drove a wedge between my spouse and me. After a while, I just gave up hope of being a mom or a wife because I felt like a failure.

So, I purchased a business and buried myself in my work 24/7. A "successful businesswoman" became my identity, and a couple of years later, I met my now-husband Bryan. He grew up in what I would define as a very religious family.

So, when we met, I was very transparent about two things that I thought would be deal-breakers:

I was an atheist

I couldn't have children

He chose to love me anyway. We ended up getting pregnant our first year together, and the day after Christmas, I held my 7-pound miracle baby girl in my arms, just staring at her and feeling this sense of joy and fulfillment. However, not long after, I held that same baby lifeless and blue in my arms, and every good feeling I had felt left my body and soul.

Nurses rushed in and were able to get her to breathe again, her color to come back, and after a month in the hospital, we got to take her home! Although she ended up ok, something inside of me broke that day, and I carried around those feelings and that pain for a good year. Every day, every night, I prepared myself to lose her, and I built up a wall between my baby girl and me and didn't allow myself to truly love her for fear of losing her.

I turned to alcohol to numb my pain and ease my worry. I got into a dark place but put on a smile every day, all while struggling between being a businesswoman or a mother as if I had to choose.

When the COVID pandemic of 2020 happened, the government shut down my job, and for the first time, I didn't have to choose between being a mom and being a businesswoman; however, I still struggled with not working because I felt insufficient not bringing in income.

One day, I saw a Monat mentor of mine, Connie Sanchez reading a book and decided to pick it up. When I opened the cover and saw a scripture, I immediately shut it and said, "Nope, not happening." I then tried to pawn it off onto my sister-in-law to read, to which she insisted that she order her own, and we read it together.

I decided to humor her and read it minus anything about Him. Which, if you know the book, that's almost impossible. On November 9th, I started reading 100 Days to Brave by Annie Downs, and on the 20th, I found God.

That morning I felt a need to re-read the prior days, even the parts about God, and that led me back to Day 7:

"You are not who you say you are or who others say you are. You are who God says you are."

I realized that I had been fighting against Him for so long, trying to be who I said I was, not who He said I was. At that moment, I got permission to just be a mom and a wife. That's who He said I was for 2020, and it took me all year to start embracing it.

Months later, on the morning of March 5th, my husband got a text from his cousin Misty Vaughn. She was inviting us over for dinner the next night (Saturday). I interrupted my husband as he read her text because I just felt I needed to tell him something more important than dinner, and I told him, "I think I'm ready to go to church."

He said, "Whaaaat?" then quickly said, "Ok! We will start looking for one."

I said, "Ok, thanks. Now, what time does Misty want us, and what can we bring?"

He said, "Let me look," and kept reading the text. When he scrolled to the end of it, Misty had also invited us to her church, Stonegate, with them on Sunday!

Bryan was beside himself that it all just came together so perfectly at that moment. I now know that God knows me well enough that it had to be MY idea, which is why He let me say it before we read the text.

That Sunday, March 7th, I walked in those doors not knowing what to expect, but I felt Him in the room, so I knew I was in a safe place.

That day Misty shared with me her "your one" card. It had my name written on it, and it was heavily worn because she had been using it as a bookmark and praying for me every single day since August 3rd, 2020.

Her prayer notecard read:

"Salvation - Holy Spirit dwell with her, mind unlocked to the knowledge of Christ." Amen.

My testimony is what set my writing in motion. I had so many strangers at the church come up to me after this, crying and hugging me, saying thank you for sharing. Even men who said they had never been through those things felt my emotion, and it even made them think differently about their wives.

People told me that God had bigger plans for me. My story and my book, Breaking the Habit of Mom Guilt, was born.

October 2021
She Felt Alone

The old me.

That girl was broken.

She was lost.

Scared.

Anxious.

She felt alone.

She was in survivor mode.

She had zero confidence.

Tried to buy her friends.

Was fake.

She drank to numb things.

She was an atheist.

She never said, "No."

She put herself last.

When I started putting myself first and focusing on myself and what I needed, everything changed.

I became a better wife.

A better mother.

A better person.

I found who I was.

I got sober.

I found God.

I realized how much women change when they become a mother and how much it affected me mentally, physically, and emotionally.

There is nothing easy about becoming a mom.

You give up a part of yourself as soon as you get pregnant, and then you also give up even more of yourself when your baby is born.

The struggle is trying to find yourself again before you completely lose yourself.

However, let me tell you from experience that trying to find who you USED to be is exactly where you lose who you have BECOME.

Becoming a mother changes you. Period.

The trick is learning to love yourself again.

A new version of you.

One that you couldn't have prepared yourself for prior because she didn't exist.

The new you can be more powerful than the old, more beautiful than when you were young, more magical than your imagination has ever known.

Embrace who you are becoming; she will always be your biggest fan.

March 2022

Seasons

As my fingers dug through cold, wet soil, making space to plant a seed, I realized a metaphor that is my life.

I push sunflower seeds deep into the soil and bury them, knowing that without this dark time, they would never see the light.

I water them daily, knowing that if I don't move my feet, they will stay in that dark place until they wither away.

I look close with each passing day, hoping that something bright and full of life pushes through the rough dark soil that has become its norm.

I wait, wanting nothing more than to smell something fresh, something new to cleanse my spirit.

I beg to hear the bees buzzing around them, spreading love from one strong and sturdy flower to the lost and almost lifeless flower next to it.

I realize that, just like this garden changes with the seasons, so do I.

I keep wanting to harvest what I have worked so hard on, but God keeps telling me, "Be patient. We aren't in that season yet."

I know now this isn't my season for harvest. It is my season to prep. Prep for what's to come.

Then, I will move my feet. I will care for, protect, and cherish what God plants in my garden.

I will follow his lead and trust that no matter what comes out of the dark soil that my life has become, He has planted something meant for me.

I will pray that it comes to fruition when He decides I am ready to receive His gift.

In this season, I don't have much to offer to others except to lead by example.

To pray while I move my feet, but to trust in His plan and His timing.

So, as I prep my garden, all I ask is that you please be gracious and respectful because my life is being renewed, and the soil I am lying in is loose, fragile, and still building up the strength to give life to everything around it.

xoxo xoxo

Writing Coach — David Strauss

David Strauss is a writing coach and editor who loves to bring people's ideas and concepts to life through the written word.

Both a creative and technical writer, David is a true wordsmith who specializes in working with people who have a compelling and transformational story that will make a difference in people's lives.

About the Author

Shila Marie was inspired to write this book through a series of life events that challenged her to closely examine who she is and what she believes.

Born to teenage parents, Shila struggled with relationships and infertility—leading to divorce. She became pregnant with her new fiancé less than a year into their relationship after being told she was infertile and then was diagnosed with skin cancer. Her coping mechanisms of alcohol and overspending failed, leading her to discover her spiritual path through Christ.

Through her challenges, she has discovered her mission and voice and has courageously made the commitment to help other moms rediscover their personal power.

This book is Shila's leap of faith to make a difference in the world.

Please help her mission by sharing this book with friends and family and by encouraging other moms to join the movement and take the challenge.

www.ingramcontent.com/pod-product-compliance
Lightning Source LLC
Chambersburg PA
CBHW060328130626
46553CB00003B/948